BUILDING YOUR RELATIONSHIP WITH

JESUS

Understanding and building your relationship with Christ

PHILLIP COMPTON

Fulton Books
Meadville, PA

Published by Fulton Books 2024

ISBN 979-8-89427-323-5 (paperback)
ISBN 979-8-89427-324-2 (digital)

Printed in the United States of America

This work is dedicated to those who have been my pillars of strength and inspiration throughout my journey.

To my dear daughter, Caitlyn, your boundless enthusiasm and unwavering belief in me have fueled my passion and commitment to my ministry. Your light guides me through the darkest of times.

To Dr. Jack Welch, a guiding light in my life, akin to the father I never had. From my earliest memories, you've imparted the teachings of God with unwavering dedication. Your love and gentle corrections have shaped me profoundly. In times of uncertainty, you were my anchor, grounding me with your wisdom. Your absence is deeply felt, especially as I embark on this new journey. I carry your memory with me always, longing for the day we will reunite. Until then, your spirit lives on within me. Thank you, and I'll see you again soon.

To Len Middleton, whose encouragement pushed me to put pen to paper and translate thoughts into words. Your belief in my abilities has been a constant source of motivation.

To Chuck Bingham, for the thought-provoking discussions and the questions that stirred my soul. Your insights have challenged me to delve deeper into my faith and understanding.

And to all the warriors for Christ, may this work serve as a beacon of light, empowering you to strengthen yourselves with the Holy Spirit and don the armor of God.

With deepest gratitude and love, Phil Compton

CONTENTS

PROLOGUE

In a world filled with distractions and uncertainties, finding a deeper connection with Jesus can bring profound peace and purpose to our lives. In *Building Your Relationship with Jesus*, author Phil Compton invites readers on a transformative journey of faith and discovery.

Drawing from personal experiences, timeless biblical wisdom, and practical insights, this book offers a road map for cultivating a meaningful relationship with Jesus Christ. Through heartfelt reflections and actionable steps, readers will explore:

- The power of prayer and spiritual disciplines to nurture intimacy with God
- Practical strategies for integrating faith into everyday life, from work to relationships
- Overcoming obstacles and doubts to experience the fullness of God's love and grace

- Deepening understanding of Scripture and its relevance to modern living
- Building a supportive community of believers for encouragement and accountability.

Whether you're seeking to renew your faith, strengthen your spiritual foundation, or embark on a journey of spiritual growth, *Building Your Relationship with Jesus* provides the guidance and inspiration you need to draw closer to the heart of God.

This morning, during my time of Bible reading and prayer, I came across Psalm 16:7–8, which struck a chord within me. Reflecting on these verses, I pondered the times when I've felt the Lord's guidance, especially in the stillness of the night. It's truly remarkable how the more we focus on Him, the more we hear from Him!

Charles Spurgeon once shared that he didn't pray for extended periods but rather made a habit of never going too long without prayer. Similarly, we all have numerous concerns occupying our minds, from family and work to everyday tasks. However, it's crucial to consciously keep the Lord at the forefront of our thoughts. Otherwise, the busyness of life can easily distract us from Him.

So take a moment now to direct your thoughts toward Jesus—praise Him, thank Him, pour out your heart to Him. Whether openly or quietly, the key is to keep Jesus always on your mind. When He occupies our thoughts, two things happen: we hear from Him more often, and He naturally becomes a part of our conversations and actions, shining through as a witness to others.

Let's commit to having Jesus at the center of our thoughts in the days ahead!

Regarding a personal experience, I received a series of verses while driving in the Midwest, which puzzled me until I later encountered them in the Bible. Each night, I prayed for understanding, and the Lord revealed it was my time. These revelations led me to write about the Holy Spirit and deepen my relationship with Christ. I hope my journey blesses and strengthens your own walk with Him. Grace and peace be with you.

CHAPTER 1

The Light

Then spake Jesus again unto them, saying, "I am the light of the world: he that followeth Me shall not walk in darkness, but shall have the light of life." (John 8:12)

As long as I am in the world, I am the light of the world. (John 9:5)

I the LORD have called thee in righteousness, and will hold thine hand, and will keep thee, and give thee for a covenant of the people, for a light of the Gentiles. (Isaiah 42:6)

Nevertheless, among the chief rulers also many believed on Him; but because of the Pharisees they did not confess Him, lest they should be put out of the synagogue: For they loved the praise of men more than the praise of God. (John 12:42–43)

That was the true light, which lighteth every man that cometh into the world. (John 1:9)

In Him was life; and the life was the light of men. (John 1:4)

Through the tender mercy of our God, whereby the dayspring from on high hath visited us. (Luke 1:78)

While ye have light, believe in the light, that ye may be the children of light. These things spake Jesus, and departed, and did hide himself from them. (John 12:36)

In whom the god of this world hath blinded the minds of them which believe not, lest the light of the glorious gospel of Christ, who is the image of God, should shine unto them. (2 Corinthians 4:4)

For God, who commanded the light to shine out of darkness, hath shined in our hearts, to give the light of the knowledge of the glory of God in the face of Jesus Christ. (2 Corinthians 4:6)

And was transfigured before them: and His face did shine as the sun, and His raiment was white as the light. (Matthew 17:2)

The same came for a witness, to bear witness of the light, that all men through Him might believe. He was not that light but was sent to bear witness of that light. (John 1:7–8)

And they that were with me saw indeed the light and were afraid; but they heard not the voice of Him that spake to me. (Acts 22:9)

Promises

No weapon that is formed against thee shall prosper; and every tongue that shall rise against thee in judgment thou shalt condemn. This is the heritage of the servants of the LORD, and their righteousness is of me, saith the LORD. (Isaiah 54:17)

Fear thou not; for I am with thee be not dismayed; for I am thy God: I will strengthen thee; yea, I will help thee; yea, I will uphold thee with the right hand of my righteousness. (Isaiah 41:10)

For I the LORD thy God will hold thy right hand, saying unto thee, Fear not; I will help thee. (Isaiah 41:13)

Thou wilt keep him in perfect peace, whose mind is stayed on thee: because he trusteth in thee. (Isaiah 26:3)

And I commanded you at that time, saying, "The LORD your God hath given you this land to possess it: ye shall pass over armed before your brethren the children of Israel, all that are meet for the war." (Deuteronomy 3:18)

These things I have spoken unto you, that in me ye might have peace. In the world ye shall have tribulation: but be of good cheer; I have overcome the world. (John 16:33)

The steps of a good man are ordered by the LORD: and he delighteth in his way.

Though he falls, he shall not be utterly cast down: for the LORD upholdeth him with His hand. (Psalms 37:23–24)

"For I know the thoughts that I think toward you," saith the LORD, "thoughts of peace, and not of evil, to give you an expected end." (Jeremiah 29:11)

And we know that all things work together for good to them that love God, to them who are the called according to His purpose. (Romans 8:28)

Faith

And all things, whatsoever ye shall ask in prayer, believing, ye shall receive. (Matthew 21:22)

For with God nothing shall be impossible. (Luke 1:37)

So then faith cometh by hearing, and hearing by the Word of God. (Romans 10:17)

Now faith is the substance of things hoped for, the evidence of things not seen. (Hebrews 11:1)

But without faith it is impossible to please Him: for he that cometh to God must believe that he is, and that he is a rewarder of them that diligently seek Him. (Hebrews 11:6)

Trust in the Lord with all thine heart; and lean not unto thine own understanding.

In all thy ways acknowledge Him, and He shall direct thy paths. (Proverbs 3:5–6)

And Jesus answering saith unto them, "Have faith in God. For verily I say unto you, that whosoever shall say unto this mountain, be thou removed, and be thou cast into the sea; and shall not doubt in his heart but shall believe that those things which he saith shall come to pass; he shall have whatsoever he saith. Therefore, I say unto you, what things soever ye desire, when ye pray, believe that ye receive them, and ye shall have them." (Mark 11:22–24)

Thou believest that there is one God; thou doest well: the devils also believe, and tremble. (James 2:19)

For we walk by faith, not by sight. (2 Corinthians 5:7)

That your faith should not stand in the wisdom of men, but in the power of God. (1 Corinthians 2:5)

Jesus said unto him, if thou canst believe, all things are possible to him that believeth. (Mark 9:23)

For whatsoever is born of God overcomes the world: and this is the victory that overcometh the world, even our faith. (1 John 5:4)

And the apostles said unto the Lord, Increase our faith. (Luke 17:5)

> But let him ask in faith, nothing wavering. For he that wavereth is like a wave of the sea driven with the wind and tossed. (James 1:6)

What to say

> But when they deliver you up, take no thought how or what ye shall speak: for it shall be given you in that same hour what ye shall speak. (Matthew 10:19)

> For the Holy Ghost shall teach you in the same hour what ye ought to say. (Luke 12:12)

> For it is not ye that speak, but the Spirit of your Father which speaketh in you. (Matthew 10:20)

> But when they shall lead you, and deliver you up, take no thought beforehand what ye shall speak, neither do ye premeditate: but whatsoever shall be given you in

that hour, that speak ye: for it is not ye that speak, but the Holy Ghost. (Mark 13:11)

Then said Jesus unto them, "When ye have lifted up the Son of man, then shall ye know that I am He, and that I do nothing of myself; but as my Father hath taught Me, I speak these things." (John 8:28)

For I have not spoken of myself, but the Father which sent Me, he gave Me a commandment, what I should say, and what I should speak. (John 12:49)

These things have I spoken unto you, being yet present with you. But the Comforter, which is the Holy Ghost, whom the Father will send in my name, he shall teach you all things, and bring all things to your remembrance, whatsoever I have said unto you. (John 14:25–26)

And they were all filled with the Holy Ghost, and began to speak with other tongues, as the Spirit gave them utterance. (Acts 2:4)

And Micaiah said, As the LORD liveth, what the LORD saith unto me, that will I speak. (1 Kings 2:14)

And thou shalt speak my words unto them, whether they will hear, or whether they will forbear for they are most rebellious. (Ezekiel 2:7)

For I will give you a mouth and wisdom, which all your adversaries shall not be able to gainsay nor resist. (Luke 21:15)

"As for Me, this is My covenant with them," saith the LORD; "My spirit that is upon thee, and My words which I have put in thy mouth, shall not depart out of thy mouth, nor out of the mouth of thy seed, nor out of the mouth of thy seed's seed," saith the LORD, "from henceforth and forever." (Isaiah 9:21)

Prayer

Hear me when I call, O God of my righteousness: thou hast enlarged me when I was in distress; have mercy upon me and hear my prayer. (Psalms 4:1)

For this shall every one that is Godly pray unto thee in a time when thou mayest be found: surely in the floods of great waters they shall not come nigh unto Him. (Psalms 32:6)

Hear my prayer, O LORD, and give ear unto my cry; hold

not thy peace at my tears: for I am a stranger with thee, and a sojourner, as all my fathers were. (Psalms 39:12)

But verily God hath heard me; he hath attended to the voice of my prayer. (Psalms 66:19)

But as for me, my prayer is unto thee, O Lord, in an acceptable time: O God, in the multitude of thy mercy, hear me, in the truth of thy salvation. (Psalms 69:13)

He will regard the prayer of the destitute, and not despise their prayer. (Psalms 102:17)

Thou shalt make thy prayer unto Him, and He shall hear thee, and thou shalt pay thy vows. (Job 22:27)

The Lord is far from the wicked: but He heareth the prayer of the righteous. (Proverbs 15:29)

Now therefore, O our God, hear the prayer of thy servant, and his supplications, and cause thy face to shine upon thy sanctuary that is desolate, for the Lord's sake. (Daniel 9:17)

When my soul fainted within me, I remembered the Lord: and my prayer came in unto thee, into thine holy temple. (Jonah 2:7)

Therefore, I say unto you, what things soever ye desire, when ye pray, believe that ye receive them, and ye shall have them. (Mark 11:24)

I pray for them: I pray not for the world, but for them which thou hast given me; for they are thine. (John 17:9)

> Likewise, the Spirit also helpeth our infirmities: for we know not what we should pray for as we ought: but the Spirit itself maketh intercession for us with groanings which cannot be uttered. (Romans 8:26)

Casting out sickness and demons

> And to have power to heal sicknesses, and to cast out devils. (Mark 3:15)

> Heal the sick, cleanse the lepers, raise the dead, cast out devils: freely ye have received, freely give. (Matthew 10:8)

> And these signs shall follow them that believe; In My name shall they cast out devils; they shall speak with new tongues. (Mark 16:17)

But if I with the finger of God cast out devils, no doubt the kingdom of God is come upon you. (Luke 11:20)

But if I cast out devils by the Spirit of God, then the kingdom of God is come unto you. (Matthew 12:28)

And the man in whom the evil spirit was leaped on them, and overcame them, and prevailed against them, so that they fled out of that house naked and wounded. (Acts 19:16)

But the Pharisees said, "He casteth out devils through the prince of the devils." (Matthew 9:34)

And Jesus rebuked the devil; and he departed out of him: and the child was cured from that very hour. (Matthew 17:18)

And he was casting out a devil, and it was dumb. And it came to pass, when the devil was gone out, the dumb spake; and the people wondered. (Luke 11:14)

Then He called his twelve disciples together, and gave them power and authority over all devils, and to cure diseases. (Luke 9:1)

Healing

He healeth the broken in heart, and bindeth up their wounds. (Psalms 147:3)

"For I will restore health unto thee, and I will heal thee of thy wounds," saith the LORD. (Jeremiah 30:17)

And ye shall serve the LORD your God, and He shall bless thy bread, and thy water; and I will take sickness away from the midst of thee. (Exodus 23:25)

Behold, I will bring it health and cure, and I will cure them, and will reveal unto them the abundance of peace and truth. (Jeremiah 33:6)

The LORD will strengthen him upon the bed of languishing: thou wilt make all his bed in his sickness. (Psalms 41:3)

O LORD my God, I cried unto thee, and thou hast healed me. (Psalms 30:2)

But when Jesus heard it, He answered him, saying, "Fear not: believe only, and she shall be made whole." (Luke 8:50)

And when Jesus saw her, He called her to him, and said unto her, "Woman, thou art loosed from thine infirmity." (Luke 13:12)

And the whole multitude sought to touch Him: for there went virtue out of Him and healed them all. (Luke 6:19)

Who his own self bare our sins in his own body on the tree, that we, being dead to sins, should live unto righteousness: by whose stripes ye were healed. (1 Peter 2:24)

Is any sick among you? Let him call for the elders of the church; and let them pray over him, anointing him with oil in the name of the Lord. (James 5:14–15)

And when He had called unto him His twelve disciples, He gave them power against unclean spirits, to cast them out, and to heal all manner of sickness and all manner of disease. (Matthew 10:1)

Do Not Fear

Be strong and of a good courage, fear not, nor be afraid of them: for the LORD thy God, He it is that doth go with thee; He will not fail thee, nor forsake thee. (Deuteronomy 31:6)

I sought the LORD, and He heard me, and delivered me from all my fears. (Psalms 34:4)

What time I am afraid, I will trust in thee.

In God I will praise His word, in God I have put my trust; I will not fear what flesh can do unto me. (Psalms 56:3–4)

The LORD is my light and my salvation; whom shall I fear? the LORD is the strength of my life; of whom shall I be afraid? (Psalms 27:1)

Peace I leave with you, my peace I give unto you: not as the world giveth, give I unto you. Let not your heart be troubled, neither let it be afraid. (John 14:27)

And the LORD said unto Joshua, "Fear not, neither be thou dismayed." (Joshua 8:1)

For God hath not given us the spirit of fear; but of power, and of love, and of a sound mind. (2 Timothy 1:7)

Be careful for nothing; but in everything by prayer and supplication with thanksgiving let your requests be made known unto God. And the peace of

God, which passeth all understanding, shall keep your hearts and minds through Christ Jesus. (Philippians 4:6–7)

There hath no temptation taken you, but such as is common to man: but God is faithful, who will not suffer you to be tempted above that ye are able; but will with the temptation also make a way to escape, that ye may be able to bear it. (1 Corinthians 10:13)

Seek the LORD and His strength, seek His face continually. (1 Chronicle 16:11)

Thou believest that there is one God; thou doest well: the devils also believe, and tremble. (James 2:19)

There is no fear in love; but perfect love casteth out fear: because fear hath torment. He that feareth is not made perfect in love. (1 John 4:18)

Fear thou not; for I am with thee: be not dismayed; for I am thy God: I will strengthen thee; yea, I will help thee; yea, I will uphold thee with the right hand of my righteousness. (Isaiah 41:10)

For I the LORD thy God will hold thy right hand, saying unto thee, "Fear not; I will help thee." (Isaiah 41:13)

CHAPTER 2

The Armor of God

The armor of God, as outlined in Ephesians 6:10–18, comprises six essential components:

1. Belt of truth
2. Breastplate of righteousness
3. Shoes of the gospel
4. Shield of faith
5. Helmet of salvation
6. Sword of the Spirit

Let's delve into each piece of this spiritual armor and understand how it empowers us as soldiers for Christ in our battle against spiritual wickedness.

1. *Belt of truth (Ephesians 6:14):* The truth serves as the foundation of the armor, holding all its pieces together. It encompasses both the truths of Scripture, which liberates us from Satan's lies, and our personal commitment to integrity and honesty.

2. *Breastplate of righteousness (Ephesians 6:14):* This righteousness, bestowed upon us by Jesus, protects our hearts from Satan's accusations. It is not our own righteousness but the righteousness of Christ covering and shielding us.

3. *Shoes of the gospel (Ephesians 6:15):* Just as soldiers need sturdy shoes for marching into battle, we require "gospel shoes" to follow Jesus obediently, overcoming obstacles with His strength and advancing the gospel.

4. *Shield of faith (Ephesians 6:16):* Above all, faith acts as our shield against Satan's attacks, deflecting doubts and temptations. This faith, a gift from God, grows as we walk with Him, enabling us to live victoriously in Christ.

5. *Helmet of salvation (Ephesians 6:17):* Protecting our minds, the helmet assures

us of our salvation, granting us peace amid Satan's deceptions. Through Jesus, we can be certain of our forgiveness and eternal life.

6. *Sword of the spirit (Ephesians 6:17):* God's Word, described as living and powerful, is our offensive weapon against the enemy. By studying and applying Scripture, we defend against temptations and defeat the devil.

7. *Prayer (Ephesians 6:18):* Though not a physical piece of armor, prayer is essential for maintaining communion with God and ensuring the effectiveness of the entire armor.

8. *Putting on the whole armor of God:* Clothing ourselves in the armor of God is synonymous with embracing a relationship with Jesus. When we surrender to Him and His righteousness, we are fully equipped to withstand Satan's schemes and stand firm in His strength.

In moments of weakness or discouragement, remember that even the weakest believer, clothed in God's invincible armor, is more than a match for the enemy. With Jesus, we are empowered to be strong and to stand against the devil's tactics.

CHAPTER 3

Understanding Jesus as the Way, the Truth, and the Life

When Jesus declared, "I am the way, the truth, and the life" (John 14:6), what did He mean? Exploring this profound statement sheds light on the essence of our faith and our journey with Christ.

In 2 Timothy 3:1–5, the Bible warns of "perilous times" in the last days. This signifies turbulent and challenging periods ahead. We are currently amidst these end times, marked by uncertainty and unrest.

In our quest for meaning, humanity seeks three fundamental aspects: guidance (the way), authenticity (the truth), and permanence (life). Jesus encapsulates these needs in His statement in John 14:6, providing answers to life's profound questions.

Let's delve into each aspect:

1. *The way*

Amidst diverse beliefs and paths, Jesus proclaims Himself as the exclusive path to God. While the world suggests multiple routes to salvation, Jesus asserts that He alone is the way. This truth may seem narrow to some, but it's a broad invitation for all to embrace. Jesus isn't merely showing the way; He is the way itself, offering salvation and reconciliation with God to all who believe.

2. *The truth*

In a world rife with deception, Jesus embodies truth. He isn't merely a purveyor of truth but truth personified. Our perception of reality often falters amidst trials, but Jesus remains steadfast as the ultimate truth. Like the disciples in the storm, we may be misled by circumstances, but Jesus reveals the truth of our situation. He dispels illusions and provides clarity, reminding us of His sovereignty overall.

3.   *The life*

Amidst temporal pursuits, Jesus offers eternal life. While worldly endeavors fade, Jesus remains the source of everlasting life and fulfillment. Material possessions and transient pleasures pale in comparison to the abundant life Jesus offers. He assures us of life beyond the transient, where our souls find eternal rest and purpose.

Jesus's proclamation reverberates through the ages, offering hope and assurance to all who heed His call. As we navigate the complexities of life, let's anchor ourselves in Jesus—the way, the truth, and the life. In Him, we find answers to life's deepest questions and fulfillment beyond measure.

Instead of seeking answers in the world's offerings, let's turn to Jesus—the ultimate source of wisdom and truth. Amidst the uncertainties of these end times, let's embrace the way, the truth, and the life found in Christ. As we journey forward, let's cling to the instruction manual of life—the Bible—for guidance and enlightenment.

4 Methods for Strengthening Your Faith

While God has endowed each person with a measure of faith (Romans 12:3), as believers, we are called to continually cultivate and nurture our faith. God desires for us not to remain stagnant but to flourish and grow in Him, progressing from one level of faith to another (Romans 1:17). Here are four practical ways to foster growth in your faith:

1. *Grow through receiving the Word*

Romans 10:17 asserts, "So then faith comes by hearing and hearing by the Word of God." To initiate growth in your faith, immerse yourself in the Word of God. As you engage with Scripture, it transforms your mindset and shapes your worldview. Consider this process as a form of "brainwashing," where your mind is cleansed and renewed by the truth of God's Word.

2. *Grow through embracing the Word*

Merely hearing the Word is insufficient; true growth occurs when you wholeheartedly believe it. Belief catalyzes a transformative experience, as evidenced by Romans 10:9–10, which outlines the confession of Jesus as Lord leading to salvation. Every aspect of your Christian journey hinges on believing God's Word, irrespective of feelings or contrary voices. Trust in the infallibility of God's promises, even amidst challenges or doubts.

3. *Grow through internalizing the Word*

After hearing and believing God's Word, the next step is to internalize it. Hold onto the truth firmly and never relinquish it. Internalization involves saturating your mind and environment with God's promises. Surround yourself with Scripture, meditate on His Word daily, and declare His truths over your life consistently. By internalizing God's Word, you anchor yourself in His promises, refusing to let go despite external pressures or doubts.

4. *Grow through applying the Word*

James 2:17–18 emphasizes the importance of aligning faith with action. Mere belief is insufficient without corresponding actions. Act on your faith by demonstrating trust in God's Word through your words and deeds. Even when circumstances seem contrary, continue to affirm God's promises and live in accordance with His truth. Your actions validate your faith and allow God's Word to manifest powerfully in your life.

By incorporating these practices—receiving, embracing, internalizing, and applying God's Word—you will experience unprecedented growth in your faith. As you diligently listen to God, believe His promises, internalize His truth, and act upon His Word, your faith will flourish, and God's transformative power will be evident in your life.

CHAPTER 5

The Potent Weapon of the Spirit
The Two-Edged Sword

Ephesians 6:16–17 admonishes believers to take up the shield of faith and the helmet of salvation, alongside the sword of the Spirit, which is the Word of God. While the armor of God is a familiar concept in spiritual warfare, the sword of the Spirit stands out as a pivotal tool in our battle against darkness. Rooted in the knowledge imparted by God's Word, this sword serves as the foundation for our spiritual armor, empowering us to combat evil forces effectively.

But what exactly is the sword of the Spirit? Hebrews sheds light on its nature and purpose:

> For the Word of God is living and active, sharper than any two-edged sword, piercing to the division of soul and of spirit, of joints and of marrow, and discerning the thoughts and intentions of the heart. And no creature is hidden from his sight but all are naked and exposed to the eyes of him to whom we must give account. (Hebrews 4:12–13)

The Word of God transcends mere text; it is imbued with divine inspiration, making it dynamic and potent. Like a two-edged sword, it penetrates deep into our being, revealing the hidden recesses of our hearts. Every time we engage with Scripture, we invite the author—the Lord Himself—into our midst. Through His Word, God delves into the depths of our souls, exposing our innermost thoughts and motives, prompting us to confront ourselves honestly before Him.

Hebrews 4 underscores that the sword of the Spirit is not solely for external battles against demonic forces; it also equips us for internal struggles against our sinful nature. As we wrestle with our inner conflicts, God's Word serves as a guiding light, leading us toward truth and righteousness.

Psalm 119 further elucidates the significance of God's Word in the lives of His people:

Focus on the Word and find delight in it: Meditate on God's precepts and statutes, cherishing His commandments with fervor.

Seek enlightenment and insight: Pray for discernment and understanding to grasp the depth of God's law.

Meditate daily: Let the Word permeate your thoughts and reflections throughout the day.

Allow the Word to direct your life: Align your actions with God's testimonies, letting His Word illuminate your path.

Treasure the Word above all: Esteem God's commandments above earthly riches, recognizing the enduring truth and righteousness they offer.

Wholehearted obedience: Hasten to obey God's commands without delay, recognizing the entirety of His Word as truth.

God has bestowed His Word upon us as a mighty weapon of the Spirit, granting us victory over the enemy. It is our duty to diligently study and obey His Word, allowing it to penetrate our hearts and guide our actions. May we heed the voice of the Lord, embracing His Word as a transformative force in our lives.

CHAPTER 6

Understanding the Significance of Believing in Jesus' Name

The first practical truth embedded in the decision to believe in the name of Jesus Christ is this: as God in human form, Jesus lived a sinless life. Even though He never said I am God, it was said in other ways like I Am and also by miracles and wonders He demonstrated while on earth. He consistently identified Himself as the Son of God. In Christianity, there is no precedent for a savior who claims to be the supreme deity. Jesus is referred to as God only in the sense that His Father has decreed all worship be directed to Jesus Christ. Though Jesus is not the Almighty God, for all intents and purposes relevant to humanity, He operates in the capacity of God. This parallels the relationship between a king who has abdicated governance of his kingdom and his son, who now rules the kingdom; both receive the same reverence from their people.

If Jesus hadn't led a sinless life, if He hadn't succeeded where Adam failed, believing in His name would serve no purpose. The devil would remain undefeated, and all our endeavors toward righteousness would be futile. As evidenced in his temptation of Jesus Christ in the wilderness, when Adam and Eve sinned, the devil gained authority to rule over the earth.

By living sinlessly, Jesus defeated the devil and earned the right to reign over the earth. In the present age, the devil's dominion is limited to the extent that people choose evil over good. If all individuals opt for goodness, the devil cannot obstruct the fruition of their virtuous choices. If you find yourself grappling with choosing what is righteous, it may signal your need for Jesus Christ.

The second practical truth stemming from faith in the name of Jesus Christ is this: in Jesus' death, the debt of sin—both spiritual and physical death—is paid. This isn't just about individual sins but encompasses all sins ever committed and those yet to be committed. Through one sacrificial death, God in Jesus Christ atoned for all sin.

What does this imply? It means the devil can no longer exact the penalty of sin from us. The price of sin has been paid, and the devil cannot demand it anymore. Furthermore, the devil cannot claim the lives of individuals as a consequence of their sins. However, if someone willingly embraces evil through deliberate choices, they effectively surrender their lives to the devil.

Consider that whether you believe in Jesus Christ or not, you have the ability to awaken from sleep only because of Jesus' sacrifice.

Upon His death, Jesus, in the Spirit, wrested from the devil the keys of death and the grave—the realm where departed souls await judgment until Jesus' crucifixion at Calvary.

While death may come for you when your time on earth concludes, the devil cannot claim you. There's a distinction here: Death acts as an agent of justice. It comes for individuals when their time is due or when they've led lives of wrongdoing and justice demands their demise. When God intervenes to spare a child from the repercussions of their parents' sinful choices, the child may perish in infancy.

The third practical truth arising from belief in Jesus Christ's name is this: through His resurrection, we gain assurance that no weakness or sin has the power to hold us captive.

When we regard ourselves as having died with Jesus Christ and risen with Him in His power, we possess the capability to conquer all sin and weaknesses.

Unless we embrace the belief that we can overcome all sin or weaknesses, we'll never actualize this reality because we'll perpetually seek to justify sin or weakness. The initial step toward harnessing the potential made possible by Jesus Christ's resurrection is acknowledging that no weakness or sin is insurmountable.

The fourth practical truth concerning belief in Jesus Christ's name is this: through His ascension, we gain access to the Holy Spirit—the ultimate objective of God's redemption of humanity through Jesus Christ.

During Christmas, people often sing, "Jesus is God's gift to the world." While this holds true to some extent, it's also misleading. Jesus is the conduit enabling God's gift to the world—the Holy Spirit. In this context, I present four scriptures, three spoken by Jesus Christ Himself and one delivered to Christians by the Holy Spirit through Apostle Paul.

Firstly Jesus affirms that every good gift anticipated by believers comes through the Holy Spirit. Secondly Jesus redeemed us so that believers could receive the Holy Spirit. Thirdly Jesus Himself asserts that He is the facilitator, not the gift itself. If Jesus is the giver of the gift, He cannot simultaneously be the gift. So how do we reconcile this with the famous John 3:16?

Whenever something is done to facilitate another, it cannot be the end of that matter. Without Jesus, we cannot receive the Holy Spirit. However, to believe in Jesus Christ without acknowledging and seeking communion with the Holy Spirit is akin to having $100 million in your bank account but lacking the means to withdraw any of it.

The fifth practical truth resulting from faith in Jesus Christ's name is this: because Jesus lives forever to intercede for believers, the blood and power of the Holy Spirit required for our cleansing from sin are always accessible through Him. Jesus' blood is perpetually available since it's His, and the Holy Spirit comes to us through Jesus Christ, ensuring its constant availability. Whenever sin proliferates in the world, the grace of God manifested in Jesus Christ multiplies even more for our salvation.

If Jesus declares that rivers of living water, which are to flow out of believers, can only come through the Holy Spirit, to believe in Jesus Christ without recognizing and embracing fellowship with the Holy Spirit is to lead a wasteful existence.

CHAPTER 7

Embracing the Significance of Engaging with Scripture

Why do you engage with the Bible? Alternatively, why do you find it challenging to connect with it? As someone deeply involved in teaching the Bible, dissecting it book by book, chapter by chapter, and line by line, it's evident to me that many Christians don't prioritize regular Bible reading. Today, I want to briefly explore why engaging in the spiritual discipline of reading the Bible consistently is crucial, how you can integrate the habit of regular Bible reading into your life, and some effective approaches to studying the Bible.

The benefits of regular Bible reading

The content we consume shapes us profoundly. Consider the impact of your daily news consumption. Regular and consistent reading of the Bible offers numerous advantages. Firstly it reveals God's character and provides His revelation to His people. Each section of the Bible showcases God's holy, unchanging, faithful, gracious, and loving nature.

Secondly, as mentioned in 2 Timothy 3:16–17, Scripture is described as "profitable for teaching, for reproof, for correction, and for training in righteousness," leading to completeness and equipping for every good work.

Thirdly regularly immersing ourselves in God's Word realigns our thinking, fostering spiritual maturity, an essential aspect of the Christian journey (Ephesians 4:14–16; Romans 12:1–2). Have you ever encountered a mature Christian who didn't engage regularly with the Bible? These reasons only scratch the surface; the benefits of regular Bible reading could be listed extensively.

Incorporating regular Bible reading into your routine

Reading the Bible is a spiritual discipline that requires dedication in our approach. If you find yourself lacking the desire to engage with Scripture, pray and ask God to ignite that passion within you. Next, carve out a dedicated time in your day for reading Scripture, making it a nonnegotiable priority. Consider finding an accountability partner or group to keep you on track with a reading plan. Initiating a reading plan with someone else might also provide mutual encouragement.

Approaching Scripture appropriately

While consistent Bible reading is a commendable practice, it's equally important to approach the Bible with care and discernment. It's easy to fall into the trap of focusing solely on application while reading Scripture. While applying the Bible to our lives is essential, sometimes our interpretations can be misguided or forced.

To avoid misinterpreting texts, it's beneficial to read verses and chapters within the context of both their immediate surroundings and the broader biblical narrative. Always seek to understand what the text reveals about God's character and nature. Consistently applying this approach will lead to a deeper understanding of God's Word. And as you grasp His Word more fully, you'll find yourself better equipped to reflect His image—a pursuit central to every Christian's journey.

CHAPTER 8

Distinguishing Mercy from Grace

In both biblical teachings and prayers, the concepts of mercy and grace frequently intersect, often leading us to perceive them as interchangeable. While there is truth to this notion, they are not entirely synonymous. Both mercy and grace emanate from God's kindness and compassion, yet they differ in their application and focus.

Grace represents God's benevolence bestowed upon us as an undeserved gift or favor. It's an expression of His inherent kindness, freely given without merit on our part. On the contrary, mercy is often associated with God's decision not to punish us for our transgressions. It entails the withholding of deserved judgment, a compassionate act that spares us from the consequences of our actions. One could envision mercy as a subset of grace, where grace encompasses all unmerited favors, and mercy specifically pertains to the absence of deserved punishment.

Scripture emphasizes that humanity, due to its inherent sinful nature, merits no favor from God (Ephesians 2:5). Everything good we experience stems from God's grace—a manifestation of His unearned favor toward us. This grace extends universally to all mankind, regardless of their spiritual state, in what is known as common grace. However, there exists a distinct form of grace known as saving grace, reserved for God's elect, providing divine assistance for their regeneration and sanctification.

Mercy, on the other hand, often manifests as deliverance from judgment in biblical narratives (Deuteronomy 4:30–31; 1 Timothy 1:13). It's the act of God's compassion that shields us from the punishment we rightfully deserve. Every day we continue to exist is a testament to God's mercy as our sinful state warrants eternal condemnation (Romans 6:23; Revelation 20:12–15). King David's plea for mercy in Psalm 51:1–2 epitomizes the human acknowledgment of dependence on God's kindness to avert deserved judgment.

The salvation offered through Jesus Christ epitomizes both mercy and grace. Despite deserving judgment, believers receive mercy through Christ, being spared from eternal condemnation. In Him, they find forgiveness, salvation, and abundant life—all manifestations of God's grace. In response, believers are called to worship and offer gratitude, approaching God's throne with confidence to receive mercy and grace in times of need (Hebrews 4:16).

CHAPTER 9

Understanding Forgiveness in the Bible

Forgiveness is a central theme in the Bible, pervading its pages from beginning to end. While the concept of forgiveness may seem straightforward, the Scriptures reveal nuanced layers to this vital aspect of our faith.

One dimension of forgiveness highlighted in the Bible is the forgiveness we receive from God due to our sin. This aspect is often at the forefront of our minds when considering forgiveness. However, the Bible also emphasizes the reciprocal nature of forgiveness within our human relationships. Our ability to forgive others is intricately linked to our growth as children of God.

What does the Bible teach about forgiveness?

Numerous Bible verses shed light on the importance of forgiving one another:

- Proverbs 10:12 emphasizes how love covers offenses and prevents strife.
- Proverbs 17:9 underscores the seeking of love by covering offenses, contrasting it with actions that lead to division.
- Genesis 50:19–21 illustrates Joseph's forgiveness toward his brothers who had wronged him, showcasing forgiveness as a means of reconciliation and compassion.
- Mark 11:25 urges forgiveness in prayer, highlighting its connection to receiving divine forgiveness.
- Luke 17:3–4 stresses the importance of continual forgiveness, even in the face of repeated offenses.
- Ephesians 4:32 and Colossians 3:12–13 urge kindness, compassion, and forgiveness toward others, mirroring God's forgiveness toward us.

Understanding forgiveness

Forgiveness can be likened to the cancellation of a debt. Just as a loan forgiven releases the debtor from obligation, forgiveness in relationships frees both parties from resentment and hostility. Holding onto grudges only poisons our own well-being while the other party may remain oblivious to the offense. Forgiveness offers liberation from toxic emotions and fosters healing.

Forgiveness is not merely a transactional act but a transformative process. It releases us from the bondage of resentment and allows us to embrace grace and compassion in our interactions.

What does Jesus teach about forgiveness?

Jesus emphasizes forgiveness within a cultural context that often prioritized legalistic interpretations of the law. He advocates for forgiveness as a means of restoring relationships and fostering love, rather than as a mere obligation to fulfill.

In Matthew 18:15–22, Jesus outlines a process for conflict resolution aimed at achieving reconciliation and forgiveness. He emphasizes the importance of limitless forgiveness, transcending legalistic boundaries.

Why does the Bible command forgiveness?

Forgiveness is both a command and a gift. It liberates us from bitterness and self-centeredness, allowing God's love to permeate our lives. Our practice of forgiveness reflects our understanding of God's forgiveness towards us.

Exceptions to forgiveness exist when genuine repentance is absent, as outlined in Matthew 18:15–20. In such cases, a temporary severance may be necessary for the protection of one's well-being and the unity of the community.

How do we practice forgiveness?

Forgiveness is a journey rather than a destination. It begins with acknowledging our shared humanity and seeking to see others through God's eyes. Seeking forgiveness involves genuine repentance and restitution while granting forgiveness requires grace and patience.

In seeking forgiveness, honesty and humility are paramount. Healing may take time, and patience is essential in fostering reconciliation.

In conclusion, forgiveness is not only a virtue but a foundational principle of Christian faith. By embracing forgiveness, we reflect God's love and invite healing and reconciliation into our lives and communities.

CHAPTER 10

The Importance of the Armor of God

Facing serious opposition

In Ephesians, Paul emphasizes the gravity of the opposition we encounter. He underscores that our struggle isn't against mere flesh and blood but against formidable spiritual forces—the rulers and authorities of this dark world (Ephesians 6:12). This depiction is intended to instill a sense of the profound reality of our adversary, the devil. In a modern context where belief in a literal devil is often scoffed at, it's crucial to recognize the tangible presence of evil in the world.

Where does this pervasive evil originate? While some may attribute it solely to human nature, the Bible offers a deeper understanding. It acknowledges the existence of unseen spiritual forces perpetuating evil in various forms.

The Ephesians, familiar with spiritual realities, were reminded of the potent opposition they faced. Similarly, we confront the same formidable adversary. Paul's language suggests that these Ephesians were accustomed to terms denoting spiritual entities, indicative of their cultural milieu. This underscores the power of the opposition, a reality we still contend with today.

The need for protection

Despite our humanity, we're enlisted in a spiritual battle against formidable adversaries. This asymmetrical conflict mirrors the struggle between hobbits and orcs in Tolkien's *Lord of the Rings*. Yet every believer is called to be a prepared soldier, equipped to withstand the spiritual onslaught.

Our battle unfolds in a world characterized by darkness—a realm where Satan's influence is pervasive. Earthly temptations, appealing to our fleshly desires, often lead us astray. Left unchecked, these forces overwhelm us, necessitating divine intervention.

Paul's exhortation to "put on the full armor of God" isn't merely a suggestion but a necessity. Satan capitalizes on the difficulty of the struggle, seeking to intimidate and coerce us into submission. Yet our defense lies in recognizing the magnitude of God's provision.

God's provision

Paul emphasizes the incomparable power available to believers—the same power that resurrected Christ from the dead. This divine power far surpasses any force arrayed against us. It's the power that conquered sin and death, elevating Christ to heavenly glory.

In light of this, we're urged to stand firm, equipped with the armor of God. This armor isn't merely symbolic but practical. Paul's strategies outline how believers can effectively utilize God's provision in their daily lives.

The Scale of God's Provision: thirty practical strategies

1. Begin each day with prayer and immersion in Scripture.
2. Commit Scripture to memory for spiritual fortification.
3. Immerse yourself in the truth of God's Word.
4. Identify faith-building activities and integrate them into your routine.
5. Avoid activities detrimental to your faith.
6. Engage in worship through song, embedding Christ's truth in your heart.
7. Seek God's strength through prayer.
8. Continually remind yourself of the gospel.
9. Share the gospel with others.
10. Maintain a spirit of prayer.
11. Depend on the Holy Spirit for guidance.
12. Analyze the enemy's tactics and prepare accordingly.
13. Anticipate and counter spiritual attacks.
14. Remain vigilant and renew your mind continually.
15. Express gratitude for salvation and victory in Christ.

16. Meditate on Christ's grace and its transformative power.
17. Find joy in God's promised triumph over evil.
18. Contemplate the future glory awaiting believers.
19. Utilize Scripture in evangelism.
20. Acknowledge your dependence on God's strength.
21. Encourage fellow believers with God's Word.
22. Foster community and mutual support.
23. Cultivate accountability relationships.
24. Intercede for fellow believers.
25. Pray for the spread of the gospel.
26. Recognize the true nature of spiritual warfare.
27. Reflect on past victories and draw strength from them.
28. Seek deeper spiritual strength and consistency.
29. Combat falsehoods with biblical truth.
30. Surrender to the Holy Spirit's control.

By embracing these strategies and relying on God's power, believers can stand firm against the schemes of the enemy.

CHAPTER 11

The Significance of Jesus' Name

It's remarkable how a single name has shaped the course of the past two thousand years, particularly in Western history. Jesus carries a sacred resonance for many, evoking a sense of holiness and divinity. Yet when Mary and Joseph first bestowed this name upon their child, it didn't carry the same weight. Although it held special meaning, Jesus was a common name during that time. Josephus, a first-century Jewish historian, mentions numerous individuals named Jesus, including four high priests. Acts 13 introduces Bar-Jesus, a Jewish false prophet, while Colossians 4 mentions Jesus Justus, a fellow worker of Paul's. Some ancient manuscripts of Matthew refer to the robber released by Pilate as Jesus Barabbas, meaning "Jesus Son of the Father."

Jesus was as ordinary a name as Jim, John, or Jerry. At its inception, there were no prayers uttered in his name, no profanity associated with it, and no hymns dedicated to it, akin to the absence of religious songs honoring individuals like John. No one could have foreseen that over the next two millennia, billions would pray in his name. However, Jesus was deliberately named. In Greek, it's Iesous; in Aramaic, Yesu, the language Jesus spoke. Both derive from the Hebrew Yeshua or Joshua, which combines "Ya," a short form of Yahweh, with "hoshea," meaning salvation. Thus, Mary and Joseph named their son Jesus, signifying "Yahweh is salvation."

Indeed, he was and remains salvation through Christ alone. Since the first Christmas, Jesus has transcended being merely a name; he embodies our sole comfort in life and death, our beacon of hope in a despairing world. Believing in Jesus Christ, the Son of God, grants life in his name (John 20:31). There exists no other name under heaven by which we can be saved (Acts 4:12). Consequently, all our actions, whether in word or deed, should be done in the name of the Lord Jesus (Colossians 3:17). God has elevated him above all, such that every knee shall bow and every tongue confess that Jesus Christ is Lord, to the glory of God the Father (Philippians 2:11–12).

However, it's vital to understand that the name of Jesus isn't a magical incantation. Mere chanting doesn't bestow special powers; the power lies in the person behind the name. In the Old Testament, names held significance beyond mere identification—they often conveyed one's essence and God's purpose for their life. Adam was the first man, Eve the mother of all living, Abraham the father of many nations, and so on.

And what about Jesus?

The angel told Joseph, "You shall call His name Jesus, for He will save his people from their sins" (Matthew 1:21). Jesus isn't just a great teacher, enlightened figure, or miracle worker. He transcends these roles to become the Savior of sinners.

"The name of Jesus dispels our fears and soothes our sorrows; it's music to the sinner's ears, bringing life, health, and peace." Such words resonate deeply. "All hail the power of Jesus' name! Let angels bow down. Crown him Lord of all with a royal diadem." These sentiments capture the essence of Jesus' name.

There's truly something extraordinary about that name. No, not merely something—everything.

CHAPTER 12

10 Reasons to Explore the Holy Spirit

Insights into the Holy Spirit

It is significant that the Word of God extensively discusses the Spirit, for God's instruction in Scripture is ample justification for delving into this truth. Nevertheless, to bolster our eagerness to delve into this topic, let's examine why studying the Holy Spirit is vital.

1. *Knowing the Spirit is understanding God*

The Holy Spirit embodies God Himself. Hence, delving into the character and deeds of the Holy

Spirit presents a remarkable opportunity to deepen our understanding of God. Nothing surpasses the value, transformative power, and life-giving essence of knowing God (Jeremiah 9:23–24; 31:33–34; John 17:3). Particularly, the Holy Spirit, as the third person of the Trinity, facilitates communion between believers and both the Father and the Son (2 Corinthians 13:14; Galatians 4:4–6). Christ assured His disciples that upon His ascension, He would not abandon them but would dwell within them alongside the Father, all through the Holy Spirit. The Holy Spirit's task is to reveal God's active presence, especially within the church.

2. *Understanding the Spirit leads to understanding salvation*

Humans cannot discern God's wisdom independently; it is through the Holy Spirit that God reveals His salvation (1 Corinthians 2:9–16). By the Spirit, sinners are reborn into the kingdom of God, for no one can confess Jesus as Lord except through the Holy Spirit (John 3:3–5; 1 Corinthians 12:3). Just as the Father decrees salvation and the Son accomplishes it, the Spirit applies salvation to individuals' lives. Through the Spirit's effective work, we become partakers of the redemption bought by Christ (John 1:11–12; Titus 3:5–6). Understanding the doctrine of the Spirit is essential for grasping how God saves sinners and determining one's salvation.

3. *Understanding the Spirit leads to understanding sanctification*

Sanctification, the process of spiritual growth in holiness, is attributed to the Spirit (2 Thessalonian 2:13; 1 Peter 1:2). The Holy Spirit universally transforms believers' natures into the image of God through Jesus Christ. All progress in holiness is directly the Spirit's doing. It is through the Holy Spirit that believers are sanctified, overcome sin, pray, receive illumination, are transformed into Christ's likeness, and glorify Christ in life and death. Essentially, every aspect of the Christian life can be attributed to the Spirit.

4. *Understanding the Spirit leads to balanced Christian living*

Christians and churches often tend to become imbalanced in their emphasis on doctrine or spiritual experience. Maintaining a balance between knowledge of doctrine and spiritual experience is vital—the balance of the Word and the Spirit. Overemphasizing either leads to intellectual coldness or emotional confusion, both of which can harden hearts and lead to skepticism. The Word and the Spirit are inseparable; the Word exists through the Spirit, and the Spirit operates through the Word. Whenever the Word is believed, it is solely due to the Spirit opening hearts to it.

5.   *Understanding the Spirit leads to right worship*

Our worship should reflect the Trinitarian nature of God as we are baptized in the name of the Father, Son, and Holy Spirit (Matthew 28:19). Worshiping one God in three persons necessitates giving equal worship to all three. Appreciating the Holy Spirit's work is crucial for worship. Under the old covenant, worship involved intricate rituals in a physical temple, revealing Christ through the Spirit (Hebrews 10:1). In the new covenant, simplicity replaces outward rituals as the church worships through Christ, with access to the Father and in one Spirit (Ephesians 2:18). The Spirit unites believers in worship despite differences, filling them with truth and joy.

6. *Understanding the Spirit honors historic Christian orthodoxy*

Christians have upheld fundamental doctrines, including the Holy Spirit's role, from the early church to the Reformation. Neglecting this doctrine means neglecting Christian heritage.

7. *Understanding the Spirit equips us for cultural engagement*

In a world where science fails to address life's deepest questions, understanding the Holy Spirit equips us to showcase Christianity's unique knowledge and spiritual experience. The Spirit's work gives Christianity a tangible, experiential dimension that sets it apart.

8. *Understanding the Spirit prepares us for spiritual warfare*

The Christian life is a battle against unseen enemies, waged with the Spirit as our supernatural ally. Just as Christ faced temptation full of the Holy Spirit, our spiritual armor and weapons are empowered by the Spirit.

9. *Understanding the Spirit highlights our dependence*

The doctrine of the Holy Spirit underscores human inability and divine sovereignty. Our dependence on the Spirit counters human pride and empowers us for God's work.

10. *Understanding the Spirit leads to knowing Christ*

Given the triune nature of God and the plan of salvation, knowing the Spirit inevitably leads to knowing Christ. The Spirit unites believers with Christ, facilitating personal communion and making believers partakers of Christ and His benefits.

CHAPTER 13

How Can One Discern the Presence of the Holy Spirit within Oneself?

According to biblical teachings, those who embrace Jesus Christ as their Lord and Savior are infused with the Holy Spirit at the moment of salvation.

> When you heard the word of truth, the gospel of your salvation, and believed in him, you were sealed with the promised Holy Spirit. He is the guarantee of our inheritance until we acquire possession of it, to the

praise of his glory. (Ephesians 1:13–14)

Being a Christian signifies having the Holy Spirit dwelling within: "You, however, are not in the flesh but in the Spirit, if in fact the Spirit of God dwells in you. Anyone who does not have the Spirit of Christ does not belong to him" (Romans 8:9).

Paul, in his teachings to the Corinthian church, emphasized the unity of believers through the Spirit: "For in one Spirit we were all baptized into one body—Jews or Greeks, slaves or free—and all were made to drink of one Spirit" (1 Corinthians 12:13). This "drinking of the Spirit" symbolizes the reception of the Holy Spirit at the moment of salvation.

Jesus, metaphorically speaking of the Spirit, invited all who are thirsty to come and drink: "'Whoever believes in me,' as the Scripture has said, 'Out of his heart will flow rivers of living water.'" Now this he said about the Spirit, whom those who believed in him were to receive" (John 7:37–39).

Therefore, if one has embraced Christ by faith, they have received the Holy Spirit. However, many believers confuse "having the Holy Spirit" with "being filled" with the Spirit. Receiving the Holy

Spirit occurs at salvation, marking believers as children of God.

Being filled with the Holy Spirit, which entails yielding to the Spirit's guidance, is an ongoing aspect of the Christian journey. "Being led by the Spirit," "walking by the Spirit," and "keeping in step with the Spirit" are all biblical expressions of the goal of Christian discipleship. Every believer should strive to be filled with the Spirit as part of their continuous communion with God.

> Do not get drunk with wine, for that is debauchery, but be filled with the Spirit, addressing one another in psalms and hymns and spiritual songs, singing and making melody to the Lord with your heart, giving thanks always and for everything to God the Father in the name of our Lord Jesus Christ. (Ephesians 5:18–20)

Some Christian denominations suggest that the baptism of the Holy Spirit is a separate experience from the indwelling that occurs at salvation. This teaching of a subsequent baptism "in fire" or "power" can lead to confusion, causing believers to doubt their possession of the Holy Spirit.

Being filled with the Holy Spirit empowers believers, fostering renewal, obedience, boldness in sharing the gospel and liberation from the bondage of sin. It results in the manifestation of the fruit of the Spirit. However, having the Holy Spirit is the hallmark of all genuine followers of Jesus Christ. In essence, if one is indeed a disciple of Jesus Christ, the Holy Spirit dwells within them.

CHAPTER 14

5 Indicators of the Holy Spirit's Presence within You

God has sent His Spirit to enact a profound transformation in our hearts, aligning them more closely with the likeness of Christ.

Recognizing our need for assistance in leading a righteous life that pleases Him, God graced us with His Spirit. Without this divine guidance, we would falter in living up to God's desires for us. As followers of Jesus Christ, we are blessed with the indwelling of the Holy Spirit.

"The Spirit of truth, whom the world cannot receive, because it neither sees Him nor knows Him; but you know Him, for He dwells with you and will be in you" (John 14:17).

Five signs indicating the presence of the Holy Spirit within you

Given that the Holy Spirit resides within us, our lives should bear witness to His presence and active influence in our hearts. Let's explore five such signs:

1) Transformation: The Holy Spirit actively works within us, fostering our growth as believers and effecting a transformation in our hearts and minds.

Titus 3:4–6 emphasizes:

> But when the kindness and love of God our Savior appeared, he saved us, not because of righteous things we had done but because of his mercy. He saved us through the washing of rebirth and renewal by the Holy Spirit, whom he poured out on us generously through Jesus Christ our Savior.

The indwelling of the Holy Spirit leads to our spiritual regeneration, making us new creations. This profound change at our core alters our behavior significantly. While the world advocates self-improvement, the Holy Spirit's work transcends that, completely renewing our being.

This transformation becomes evident to others. When someone embraces salvation, observers often witness a remarkable change, though they may not grasp its cause. A person filled with the Holy Spirit undergoes a profound metamorphosis, reflecting God's glory.

2) Growth in the fruit of the spirit: An unmistakable sign of the Holy Spirit's presence is the manifestation of the fruit of the Spirit.

Galatians 5:22–23 outlines: "But the fruit of the Spirit is love, joy, peace, forbearance, kindness, goodness, faithfulness, gentleness, and self-control. Against such things there is no law."

As we spend time with God, we naturally grow in love, joy, peace, and the other fruits listed in this scripture. Observing someone's growth in the fruit of the Spirit indicates their openness to God's transformative work in their hearts.

The journey of salvation is ongoing, and it takes time for these fruits to fully blossom in our lives. Sometimes, we may find ourselves lacking in joy or kindness, but through prayer, we can seek God's assistance. Patience is key as we develop in the fruit of the Spirit. As these traits manifest, our internal source of joy and happiness shifts.

3) Guidance by the Holy Spirit: With the Holy Spirit dwelling within us, we can heed His guidance in our daily lives.

Those filled with the Holy Spirit often speak of God's communication and guidance, receiving direction for every step they take. God desires our obedience to His Word, and following His Spirit's promptings leads us in the right direction.

"For those who are led by the Spirit of God are the children of God" (Romans 8:14).

Believers led by the Holy Spirit align themselves with God's will and direction. God communicates with us internally, guiding our paths. In moments of uncertainty, seeking the Holy Spirit's guidance yields clarity and reduces mistakes. Understanding God's will requires attentiveness to His Spirit, leading to wise and righteous decisions.

4) Speaking in tongues: One of many indications of being filled with the Holy Spirit is the ability to speak in tongues. This seems to be the most common. Keep in mind if you don't, it does not mean you are not filled.

After salvation, believers may experience the baptism of the Holy Spirit, resulting in speaking in tongues.

"They saw what seemed to be tongues of fire that separated and came to rest on each of them. All of them were filled with the Holy Spirit and began to speak in other tongues as the Spirit enabled them" (Acts 2:3–4).

Jesus promised believers the ability to speak in new tongues. "And these signs will accompany those who believe: In My name, they will drive out demons; they will speak in new tongues" (Mark 16:17).

While speaking in tongues is not a prerequisite for salvation, it signifies the baptism of the Holy Spirit.

5) Discernment of spirits: A hallmark of the Holy Spirit's presence is a discerning spirit, evaluating teachings against the truth of God's Word.

Believers are urged to test the spirits to discern their authenticity.

"Dear friends, do not believe every spirit, but test the spirits to see whether they are from God, because many false prophets have gone out into the world" (1 John 4:1).

Those filled with the Holy Spirit readily identify false teachings and prophets, relying on the Word of God for confirmation. Studying and internalizing the Bible safeguards against deception, preserving the truth of faith.

Conclusion

These five signs are just a glimpse of the Holy Spirit's presence within a person. Through intimate communion with God, one can discover additional signs.

To continually experience the Holy Spirit's fullness, make room for Him in your heart, allowing Him to work mightily within you.

God accomplishes His purposes on earth through the Holy Spirit, renewing our hearts and guiding us toward godliness and righteousness.

CHAPTER 15

Identifying Spiritual Walk

In Galatians 5:16, Paul urges believers to walk by the Spirit. Sounds simple, but it's often easier said than done. How can we discern whether our actions are truly guided by the Spirit or not? Humans are adept at convincing themselves they're living spiritually when they're far from it.

Contrasting the life led by the Spirit with the life of the sinful nature, we find markers outlined in Galatians 5:22–23: "But the fruit of the Spirit is love, joy, peace, patience, kindness, goodness, faithfulness, gentleness, self-control; against such things, there is no law." Years ago, I resolved to embody these qualities, recognizing them as vital attributes. Yet I soon realized their depths of meaning were far richer than I initially grasped.

Two indicators of walking in the Spirit

While I'm still on the journey of understanding, two principles have proven helpful in my pursuit of a Spirit-led life.

1. *Alignment with God's Word:* The Spirit of God always aligns with the Word of God. Delving into Scripture reveals its timeless truth and applicability. For instance, my understanding of "love" evolved as I encountered its various expressions in the Bible. God's love, displayed through Jesus, is the ultimate standard. It's gracious, merciful, and patient. When I'm tempted to react in anger, Scripture reminds me to temper my response (Ephesians 4:26, 29). By comparing my actions to God's Word, I discern whether they're Spirit led.

2. *Embracing freedom:* At a retreat focused on the fruit of the Spirit, we initially felt overwhelmed by the standard set before us. However, we realized we couldn't produce these qualities on our own. True fruit of the Spirit isn't borne of human effort but flows from surrender to God's power. Recognizing

this brought a sense of freedom from striving and condemnation. Our desire to embody these traits is evidence of the Spirit's presence within us (Romans 8:5).

Balancing work and the Spirit's guidance

Striving to live by Spirit-inspired attributes isn't a replacement for the Spirit's work but a response to it (Romans 8:5). Despite our inherent flaws and the challenges of living in a fallen world, we can trust the Holy Spirit's guidance. Though we may stumble, God's grace sustains us, and His Spirit empowers us to walk in step with Him (Galatians 5:25).

Understanding Blasphemy against the Holy Spirit

Blasphemy against the Holy Spirit is referenced in three of the four gospels: Matthew 12:22–32, Mark 3:22–30, and Luke 12:10. Many Christians grapple with fears of having committed this sin or worry about doing so in the future. Therefore, it's crucial to delve into what Jesus meant by this concept.

1. *The context of Jesus' miracles:* In Matthew 12, Jesus performs a miracle by healing a blind and mute man. The undeniable nature of this miracle leaves no room for doubt. Yet the religious leaders attribute

Jesus' power to Satan, refusing to acknowledge it as God's work.

2. *Understanding Satan's kingdom:* Jesus explains that Satan wouldn't act against his own interests by empowering Jesus. Rather, Jesus represents a force stronger than Satan, aiming to liberate humanity from spiritual bondage.

3. *The nature of the unforgivable sin:* Jesus clarifies that all sins, even those against him, are forgivable except blasphemy against the Holy Spirit. But what constitutes this "eternal sin"?

4. *Sin against the Holy Spirit:* The religious leaders' sin wasn't against Jesus but against the Spirit who empowered his miracles. They knowingly attributed divine works to the devil.

5. *Severity of the sin:* Blasphemy against the Holy Spirit isn't mere disbelief but a willful rejection of undeniable truth. It's a persistent defiance, declaring divine acts as demonic.

6. *Defiance beyond repentance:* This sin isn't unforgivable due to limitations in God's grace but because it renders repentance

impossible. It arises from a calloused heart resistant to conviction.

7. *Repentance and forgiveness:* Forgiveness is contingent upon repentance. Blasphemy against the Holy Spirit indicates a heart hardened against repentance.

8. *Assurance of forgiveness:* Those ashamed of their sin, feeling conviction, or fearing they've committed the unforgivable sin likely haven't. True repentance precludes this sin.

9. *The role of forgiveness:* Ultimately, God's forgiveness is what matters. Trusting in Christ as the source of forgiveness assures one hasn't committed blasphemy against the Holy Spirit.

In summary, while understanding the concept of blasphemy against the Holy Spirit is vital, true repentance and trust in Christ ensure forgiveness is always attainable.

CHAPTER 17

Is it Expected for a Believer to Sense the Presence of the Holy Spirit?

While certain aspects of the Holy Spirit's work may elicit a feeling, such as conviction of sin, comfort, and empowerment, Scripture doesn't direct us to gauge our connection with the Holy Spirit solely on our feelings. Every believer who is born again receives the indwelling of the Holy Spirit. Jesus assured us of this when he said that the Comforter would come to be with us and within us.

> And I will ask the Father, and He will give you another advo-

cate to help you and be with you forever—the Spirit of truth. The world cannot accept Him because it neither sees Him nor knows Him. But you know Him, for He lives with you and will be in you. (John 14:16–17)

In essence, Jesus is sending one akin to Himself to be present with us and within us.

We acknowledge the Holy Spirit's presence because God's Word affirms it. Every born-again believer is indwelt by the Holy Spirit, yet not every believer is under the control of the Holy Spirit, and there lies a distinct difference. When we act according to our fleshly desires, we are not operating under the Holy Spirit's control despite His indwelling presence. The Apostle Paul elucidates on this truth, employing an illustration to aid our understanding. "Do not get drunk on wine, which leads to debauchery. Instead, be filled with the Spirit" (Ephesians 5:18). Many interpret this verse as a warning against excessive drinking, but its context concerns the conduct and warfare of a Spirit-filled believer. Hence, there's more here than a caution about alcohol consumption.

When people indulge excessively in wine, they display certain traits: clumsiness, slurred speech, impaired judgment. The Apostle Paul draws a parallel here. Just as certain traits identify someone under the influence of alcohol, there should also be identifiable traits of someone under the control of the Holy Spirit. In Galatians 5:22–24, we learn about the "fruit" of the Spirit, manifested in the life of a believer under His control.

The verb tense in Ephesians 5:18 implies an ongoing process of "being filled" by the Holy Spirit. Since it's an exhortation, it implies the possibility of not being filled or controlled by the Spirit. The subsequent verses in Ephesians 5 outline the characteristics of a Spirit-filled believer:

> Speaking to one another with psalms, hymns, and spiritual songs. Sing and make music in your heart to the Lord, always giving thanks to God the Father for everything, in the name of our Lord Jesus Christ. Submit to one another out of reverence for Christ. (Ephesians 5:19–21)

We are filled with the Spirit not because we feel so, but because it's the privilege and possession of a Christian. Being filled or controlled by the Spirit results from obedience to the Lord, a gift of grace rather than an emotional sentiment. Emotions can deceive, leading us into a frenzy of the flesh rather than the Spirit. "So I say, walk by the Spirit, and you will not gratify the desires of the flesh… Since we live by the Spirit, let us keep in step with the Spirit" (Galatians 5:16).

Nevertheless, there are instances when we might be overwhelmed by the presence and power of the Spirit, often evoking an emotional response. In such moments, it's a joy unlike any other. King David "danced with all his might" (2 Samuel 6:14) when the Ark of the Covenant was brought to Jerusalem. Experiencing joy through the Spirit is understanding that as children of God, we are blessed by His grace. Hence, the ministries of the Holy Spirit can indeed involve our emotions. Yet we're cautioned not to base our assurance of possessing the Holy Spirit solely on our feelings.

CHAPTER 18

Paraclete (The Holy Spirit) Deep Study Part 1

Ministry to believers

> When he, the Spirit of truth, comes, he will guide you into all truth. He will not speak on his own; he will speak only what he hears, and he will tell you what is yet to come. He will bring glory to me by taking from what is mine and making it known to you. (John 16:13–14)

Prior to Jesus' crucifixion, he assured his disciples that both he and the Father would send them "another Counselor" (John 14:16, 26; 15:26; 16:7). The term "counselor" or "Paraclete"—derived from the Greek word "*parakletos*" meaning supporter—denotes a helper, adviser, strengthener, encourager, ally, and advocate. The term "another" indicates that Jesus, the initial Paraclete, was promising a successor who would continue his teachings and testimonies after his departure (John 16:6–7).

The ministry of the Paraclete is inherently personal and relational, implying the complete personhood of the one fulfilling it. Although the Old Testament extensively describes the Spirit's involvement in Creation (e.g., Genesis 1:2; Psalm 33:6), revelation (e.g., Isaiah 61:1–6; Micah 3:8), empowerment for service (e.g., Exodus 31:2–6; Judges 6:34; 15:14–15; Isaiah 11:2), and inner renewal (e.g., Psalm 51:10–12; Ezekiel 36:25–27), it does not explicitly state that the Spirit is a distinct divine person.

In the New Testament, however, it becomes evident that the Spirit is just as much a distinct person from the Father as the Son is. This is evident not only from Jesus' promise of "another Counselor" but also from the Spirit's actions, including speaking (Acts 1:16; 8:29; 10:19; 11:12; 13:2; 28:25), teaching (John 14:26), bearing witness (John 15:26), searching (1 Corinthians 2:11), making decisions (1 Corinthians 12:11), interceding (Romans 8:26–27), being lied to (Acts 5:3), and capable of being grieved (Ephesians 4:30). These attributes can only be attributed to a personal being.

The divinity of the Spirit is apparent from the assertion that lying to the Spirit is lying to God (Acts 5:3–4) and from the association of the Spirit with the Father and the Son in blessings (2 Corinthians 13:14; Revelations 1:4–6) and in the baptismal formula (Matthew 28:19). The Spirit is referred to as "the seven spirits" in Revelation 1:4; 3:1; 4:5; 5:6, partly because seven symbolizes divine perfection and partly because the Spirit ministers in fullness.

Therefore, the Spirit is referred to as "he," not "it," and must be revered, loved, and obeyed alongside the Father and the Son.

The central ministry of the Paraclete is to testify to Jesus Christ, glorifying Him by revealing His nature to His disciples (John 16:7–15) and making them aware of their identity in Him (Romans 8:15–17; Galatians 4:6). The Spirit enlightens (Ephesians 1:17–18), regenerates (John 3:5–8), guides into holiness (Romans 8:14; Galatians 5:16–18), transforms (2 Corinthians 3:18; Galatians 5:22–23), provides assurance (Romans 8:16), and equips for ministry (1 Corinthians 12:4–11). All the work of God within us—shaping our hearts, characters, and behavior—is accomplished by the Spirit, although certain aspects are sometimes attributed to the Father and the Son, whom the Spirit serves.

The full ministry of the Paraclete began on the morning of Pentecost, following Jesus' ascension (Acts 2:1–4). John the Baptist had prophesied that Jesus would baptize with the Spirit (Mark 1:8; John 1:33), in accordance with the Old Testament promise of a pouring out of God's Spirit in the last days (Joel 2:28–32; cf. Jeremiah 31:31–34), and Jesus had reiterated this promise (Acts 1:4–5). Pentecost morning held a twofold significance: it marked the beginning of the final era of world history before Christ's return and represented a significant enhancement of the Spirit's ministry and the experience of being connected to God compared to the Old Testament era.

Jesus' disciples were evidently believers born of the Spirit prior to Pentecost, so their Spirit baptism, which empowered their lives and ministries (Acts 1:8), did not mark the beginning of their spiritual journey. However, for all who have believed since Pentecost, starting with the converts on that day, receiving the Spirit in full new-covenant blessing has been an integral part of their conversion and spiritual birth (Acts 2:37; Romans 8:9; 1 Corinthians 12:13). All subsequent capacities for service in a Christian's life should be understood as flowing from this initial Spirit baptism, which intimately unites the believer with the risen Christ.

CHAPTER 19

Divine Endowments of the Holy Spirit Deep Study Part 2

Empowerment by the Spirit

> However, each of us has received grace in accordance with the measure of Christ's gift...
>
> He...appointed some to be apostles, some to be prophets, some to be evangelists, and some to be pastors and teachers, to equip His people for works of service, so that the body of Christ may be built up. (Ephesians 4:7, 11–12)

The New Testament portrays local churches where certain Christians hold formal and official ministerial positions (such as elder overseers and deacons, Philippians 1:1) while all members engage in informal acts of service. The ideal in the New Testament is for every member to minister within the body of Christ. It's evident that those in formal roles should not hinder informal ministries but should instead facilitate them (Ephesians 4:11–13). Similarly, those engaging in informal ministry should respect the authority of overseers, ensuring that their actions contribute to order and edification (1 Corinthians 14:3–5, 12, 26, 40; Hebrews 13:17). As each part of the body of Christ fulfills its role (Ephesians 4:16) and carries out its unique form of service (Ephesians 4:7, 12), the body grows in maturity in faith and love.

The term "gift" (literally meaning *donation*) is mentioned in relation to spiritual service only in Ephesians 4:7–8. Paul interprets the phrase "He… gave gifts to men" as referring to Christ, after His ascension, bestowing individuals upon His church who are called and equipped for roles such as apostles, prophets, evangelists, and pastor-teachers. Through the empowering ministry of these individuals, Christ assigns a ministry role to every Christian. In other passages (Romans 12:4–8; 1 Corinthians

12–14), Paul refers to these divinely given abilities as "*charismata*" (gifts which are specific manifestations of "*charis*" or grace, God's active and creative love, 1 Corinthians 12:4) and also as "*pneumatika*" (spiritual gifts as specific demonstrations of the energy of the Holy Spirit, God's "*pneuma*," 1 Corinthians 12:1).

Despite various uncertainties and debated topics surrounding New Testament charismata, three certainties emerge. First a spiritual gift is an ability to express, celebrate, and demonstrate Christ in some manner. It's emphasized that gifts, when used correctly, edify Christians and churches. Since knowledge of God in Christ is what truly edifies, each gift must enable one to show and share Christ in an edifying manner.

Second gifts come in two types: those related to speech and those related to practical acts of love and assistance. In Romans 12:6–8, Paul's list of gifts alternates between these categories: prophecy, teaching, and exhortation are gifts of speech while serving, giving, leading, and showing mercy are gifts of practical assistance. This alternation suggests that no gift is superior to another; despite differences in function, all gifts are equally dignified, and the key is to properly use the gift one possesses (1 Peter 4:10–11).

Third no Christian is without a gift (1 Corinthians 12:7; Ephesians 4:7), and it's the responsibility of each individual to discover, develop, and fully utilize the capacities for service that God has bestowed upon them.

CHAPTER 20

What is the Significance of Baptism?

Baptism in water signifies a believer's complete trust in and reliance on Jesus Christ, along with a dedication to obediently live according to His teachings. It also symbolizes unity with all believers worldwide, expressing solidarity with every member of the body of Christ. However, it's crucial to understand that baptism does not grant salvation; rather, salvation comes through grace by faith, independent of deeds. We undergo baptism in obedience to Jesus' command: "Go therefore and make disciples of all nations, baptizing them in the name of the Father and the Son and the Holy Spirit" (Matthew 28:19).

Water baptism is reserved for believers who recognize their need for salvation due to sin and accept Jesus Christ as their Savior, believing in His death, burial, and resurrection. This faith results in spiritual rebirth through the Holy Spirit, ensuring eternal salvation and a life dedicated to Christ. Baptism serves as a powerful symbol of our identification with Christ's death and resurrection, illustrating our freedom from sin and our new life in Him. Additionally, it mirrors the spiritual purification experienced through salvation, analogous to the cleansing of the flesh by water.

The example of the repentant thief on the cross, who received salvation without undergoing water baptism, illustrates that baptism is not a prerequisite for salvation. Despite his lack of baptism, he was spiritually united with Christ's death and received the promise of eternal life through faith alone.

As followers of Christ, we are called to be baptized in water as an act of obedience and love for Him. Immersion baptism is the scriptural method, symbolizing the profound truth of Christ's death, burial, and resurrection.

CHAPTER 21

Exercising Authority
over Angels

In contemporary society, there is a deep fascination with angels, leading to the field of study known as "angelology." Angels find representation in various forms, from ornaments and seasonal decorations to cinematic and televised portrayals. Within Christianity, divergent beliefs exist regarding the extent of human authority over angels, with some asserting the ability to command them, including their direction over angels and even demons in the name of Jesus.

However, it is crucial to discern the scriptural basis for such claims. Nowhere in the Bible do we find instances of humans commanding angels, either under their own authority or in the name of Jesus. Indeed, there are no passages suggesting that humanity possesses control over the actions of angels. Jesus, in fact, voluntarily assumed a position lower than that of angels to experience human suffering (Hebrews 2:7–9; Psalm 8:4–5).

The assertion that believers hold dominion over angels is unfounded. Several biblical principles affirm that angels operate under God's command, not human authority:

- When the Israelites cried out to the Lord, He responded by sending an angel to deliver them from Egypt (Numbers 20:16). It was not at the Israelites' command but at God's decree that the angel intervened.
- In the account of Shadrach, Meshach, and Abednego, it was God who sent His angel to rescue them from the fiery furnace (Daniel 3:17–18, 28). The three did not summon the angel; rather, God acted on their behalf.
- Similarly, when Peter was imprisoned, it was the prayers of the church in Jerusalem that led to his miraculous deliverance, facilitated by an angel sent by the Lord (Acts

12:5, 11). There was no human command involved in this intervention.

Angels are described as "holy angels" who execute God's will, not human desires (Mark 8:38; Revelation 14:10). Therefore, the idea of humans exercising authority over angels lacks biblical support.

CHAPTER 22

Understanding the Pretribulation Rapture

Various interpretations exist regarding the timing of the Rapture, with the Pretribulation Rapture being a prominent belief held by many. While proponents passionately defend their stance using Scripture, it's important to remember God's call for unity and peace among believers. This directive should guide our discussions on eschatological matters, the study of last things.

While opinions may differ on specific details, all Christians agree on key aspects of Christ's second coming:

- His return will be sudden, personal, and visible.

- We are to eagerly anticipate His return.
- The exact timing of His coming remains unknown to us.
- His return will bring judgment.

To delve into the concept of the Pretribulation Rapture, it's crucial to unpack the meaning of each component term within this belief system.

Tribulation: Referenced in Matthew 24:21, the tribulation is often associated with the seven-year period described in Daniel 9:24–27. Divided into two parts, the first half is relatively peaceful while the second, known as the Great Tribulation, is a time of unprecedented distress.

Pretribulation: this refers to the belief that the Rapture will occur before the onset of the Tribulation, as outlined in passages like Matthew 24:21 and 1 Corinthians 15:51–53.

Rapture: Although not explicitly termed in Scripture, the concept is drawn from 1 Thessalonians 4:16–17, where believers are described as being caught up to meet the Lord. The Greek word *"harpazo,"* translated as "caught up," conveys the idea of being snatched away swiftly.

Combining these definitions, the Pretribulation Rapture doctrine asserts that believers will be taken up to be with Jesus prior to the period of divine wrath during the tribulation.

Proponents of this view argue that it:

—   encourages holy living in an increasingly secular world
—   highlights the importance of evangelism
—   fosters a passion for global missions

Different perspectives on the timing of the Rapture stem from varying interpretations of the millennium, the thousand-year reign of Christ mentioned in Revelation 20:1–4. These include:

—   *Amillennialism:* interprets the millennium figuratively, emphasizing Jesus' reign between His two advents.
—   *Premillennialism:* believes in Christ's return to remove His church before the tribulation.
—   *Postmillennialism:* envisions a worldwide conversion to Christianity culminating in Christ's return.

These views align with different timings of the Rapture: pretribulation, midtribulation, and post-tribulation, each with its own rationale and scriptural basis.

Supporters of the Pretribulation Rapture cite passages such as 1 Corinthians 15:51–53 and 1 Thessalonians 4:13–18, emphasizing the removal of believers before the onset of divine wrath.

However, opponents present counterarguments, pointing to passages like 1 Thessalonians 4:17 and Matthew 24:15–28, which suggest a visible and post-tribulation return of Christ.

Ultimately, while we may present our cases and cite various scriptures, the final authority rests with God's Word. It's essential to approach these discussions with humility, relying on the guidance of the Holy Spirit.

As we await Christ's return, our focus should not be solely on deciphering the timing of eschatological events but on faithfully obeying God's commands and sharing the Gospel with others. In the end, our duty is summed up in Ecclesiastes 12:13: to fear God and keep His commandments.

CHAPTER 23

Is the War of Ezekiel 38 the Same as Armageddon?

Undoubtedly, Armageddon signifies a significant international assault on Israel, specifically Jerusalem, at the culmination of the tribulation period with Jesus Christ directly intervening to defend Israel. While there are overarching similarities between these two conflicts, it is the divergences that are pivotal in determining whether they are identical.

The primary distinction lies in the origins of the invading forces. Ezekiel identifies specific nations involved, suggesting a regional conflict, whereas at Armageddon, it is stated that the Lord will gather all nations against Jerusalem for battle, indicating a global engagement. This divergence is substantial.

Secondly Ezekiel's invasion originates from the north, whereas the assault at Armageddon encompasses forces from across the entire earth.

Thirdly Ezekiel portrays Israel as being in a state of security and rest, contrasting starkly with the perilous circumstances preceding Armageddon at the end of the tribulation.

Fourthly, while Ezekiel's prophecy emphasizes divine intervention through natural upheaval, Armageddon depicts a direct battle between the Lord and the assembled nations, culminating in the victory of the King of Kings.

Fifthly the motivations behind the invasions differ: Ezekiel's invaders seek spoil, whereas the purpose of the Armageddon campaign is the destruction of the Jewish people.

Sixthly Ezekiel mentions a protest against the invasion, which is absent in the context of the Armageddon campaign, where all nations are involved.

Seventhly the timing between the campaigns allows for distinct events such as the burial of the dead and the disposal of war implements, indicating separate occurrences.

Moreover, at Armageddon, the beast leads the invasion while in Ezekiel's prophecy, Gog heads the invading force.

Lastly the armies assembled at Armageddon directly oppose Jesus Christ, unlike Ezekiel's northern military coalition.

These distinctions suggest that the war of Ezekiel 38 and Armageddon are separate events.

CHAPTER 24

Understanding the
Bottomless Pit

The term "bottomless pit" originates from the Greek in the New Testament, where it is rendered as one word and denotes the "abyss," signifying a boundless, unfathomable depth. In Roman mythology, a similar concept exists in Orcus, a profound chasm within the depths of the earth, serving as a realm for the departed and, notably, as the domain of demons. In Revelation 9:1–12, the bottomless pit houses a distinctive breed of demon and is also the lair of the beast engaged in conflict with the two witnesses (Revelation 11:7–8). During the onset of the millennial kingdom, it becomes the confinement for Satan (Revelation 20:1–3). However, at the conclusion of the thousand years, Satan is freed, instigating an unsuccessful rebellion against God (Revelation 20:7–10).

The bottomless pit may be linked with a place referred to as Tartarus, a term used only once in Scripture, in 2 Peter 2:4, signifying a place of incarceration for "angels who sinned," held in darkness awaiting judgment. Tartarus, akin to the abyss, is depicted as dismal dungeons in the NIV translation. These same angels are mentioned in Jude 6 as those who "abandoned their own home" (Genesis 6:2).

If Tartarus equates to the abyss, then its denizens are likely the fallen angels who transgressed and departed from their original abode. The bottomless pit serves as a holding ground for the most nefarious of angels, including Satan himself and those who endeavored unsuccessfully to thwart God's plan before the Flood (Genesis 3:15). These inmates of the abyss are temporarily released during the final three and a half years of the tribulation to execute God's decree of torment upon the wicked (Revelation 9:5). Despite their malevolent intent to annihilate humanity, God maintains control over their terror and restricts their power.

CHAPTER 25

The Authority of Jesus and the Future Resurrection

In Revelation 1:18, Jesus declares his supremacy over death and Hades, emphasizing his control and authority. He asserts this authority in John 10:17–18, indicating his power to lay down his life and take it up again. When Jesus died, it was according to his own timing, showcasing his unique authority over death. Just as giving someone "the key to the city" symbolizes honor and access, possessing the "keys of death" signifies Jesus' ultimate authority over life and death.

Similarly, in Isaiah 37:2, Eliakim is granted authority symbolized by the key to the house of David, highlighting his position of power. Revelation further depicts an angel given control over the bottomless pit, demonstrating the significance of possessing keys as representing authority or control.

The concept of eternal life through Jesus Christ is emphasized in 1 John 5:6–13, where Jesus' possession of the keys of death signifies his power to grant salvation and release believers from death.

The Rapture and the millennial reign

Various interpretations exist regarding the second coming of Jesus Christ, with some believing in a two-phase event: first the secret rapture of believers, followed by a period of tribulation, and then Christ's return to reign on earth for a thousand years with his saints. Others believe in a single event where Christ's return and the Rapture occur after the tribulation.

While Christians may disagree on the details, the common belief is in the bodily, visible return of Christ to rule and reign with his saints. The specifics of these events are yet to be fully revealed, but the certainty of Christ's return remains a foundational belief.

The state of the soul after death

Death prompts questions about the fate of the soul, but Scripture provides assurance that believers immediately enter the presence of God upon death. The concept of "soul sleep," suggesting unconsciousness until the final resurrection, is refuted by passages like 2 Corinthians 5:6–8 and Philippians 1:21–24, which depict believers' immediate presence with Christ after death.

Jesus' promise to the thief on the cross, along with biblical events like the stoning of Stephen and the transfiguration, affirm the conscious and immediate presence of believers with God after death. The story of Lazarus and the rich man underscores the idea of consciousness after death, rejecting the notion of soul sleep.

Scripture suggests believers will have intermediate bodies until the resurrection, similar to Jesus' resurrected body. While details about these bodies remain mysterious, believers can find comfort in the certainty of resurrection and the promise of eternal life with Christ.

In conclusion, while questions about death may provoke fear, Scripture offers assurance and hope for believers, emphasizing the immediate presence with God after death and the promise of resurrection and eternal life.

CHAPTER 26

Distinguishing between Hell and the Lake of Fire

In the book of Revelation, John introduces a significant location known as the Lake of Fire. While this fiery abyss is only mentioned toward the end of the Bible, its relevance to Christians is profound, serving as a reminder of the consequences of sin, the redemption offered through Jesus, and the imperative to spread the gospel. Let's explore five biblical truths concerning this fiery realm.

1. *Eternal consequences for rejecting Christ*

According to Revelation 20, unbelievers will face God's judgment at the Great White Throne, where those not found in the Lamb's Book of Life will be cast into the Lake of Fire, enduring everlasting punishment. Despite alternative interpretations suggesting annihilation or corrective punishment, Scripture supports the notion of eternal torment for those in the Lake of Fire, alongside the Antichrist, false prophet, and Satan.

2. *Distinctiveness of the Lake of Fire from hell*

While some equate the Lake of Fire with hell, there are clear distinctions. Presently, no one resides in the Lake of Fire; rather, it awaits future occupants after the Great White Throne Judgment. Hell, represented by Sheol and Hades, serves as a temporary abode for the unsaved, destined to be cast into the Lake of Fire, similar to how heaven is an interim dwelling for believers.

3. *Primacy of the Antichrist and false prophet*

Although the Lake of Fire was originally designated for Satan and his cohorts, the Antichrist and false prophet will be its initial inhabitants. Following their failed rebellion against Christ, they will face defeat and subsequent punishment in the Lake of Fire, setting the stage for Satan's ultimate condemnation.

4. *Varied degrees of punishment*

At the Great White Throne Judgment, unbelievers will undergo differing levels of punishment based on their deeds. While this judgment doesn't determine salvation, it underscores the rejection of Jesus' offer of eternal life, leading to varying consequences in the Lake of Fire.

5. *Satan's ultimate destiny*

A crucial aspect concerning the Lake of Fire is its role as Satan's eternal destination. Contrary to popular depictions, Satan currently roams the earth, opposing God's plan. However, his defeat is inevitable as Jesus will cast him into the fiery abyss following his final rebellion, fulfilling Scripture's promise of his ultimate demise.

Why it matters

Though the notion of eternal torment may discomfort many, biblical truth emphasizes the reality of consequences for rejecting salvation. Rather than allowing emotions to dictate our understanding, we're called to trust in Scripture and actively share the gospel with others.

CHAPTER 27

The Aftermath of the Rapture

What happens after the Rapture?

After the Rapture occurs, questions arise regarding the fate of Christians remaining on earth. The Rapture, described as the gathering of believers to meet Christ in the air (1 Thessalonians 4:16–17), precedes the Day of the Lord, which marks the beginning of the tribulation period (Daniel 9:27). This suggests that immediately following the Rapture, no Christians will remain on earth as they will have all been taken away. The subsequent events shed light on the developments following the Rapture.

Events following the Rapture: According to 1 Thessalonians 4:16–5:2, the Day of the Lord begins after the Rapture, emerging unexpectedly like a thief in the night. The precise timing of this event remains unknown, adding an element of surprise. This distinguishes it from scenarios where the Rapture occurs in the middle or at the end of the tribulation, where the predictable duration of the tribulation (seven years) prevents the Day of the Lord from being sudden. This message is conveyed in 1 Thessalonians 5:2–3 and Daniel 9:27.

As indicated in 1 Thessalonians 4:3, the Day of the Lord commences with a period of peace, marking the start of the tribulation, which later descends into destruction after 3.5 years. References in Joel 2:31 to the Day of the Lord and Joel 3:9–17 describing the tribulation include events like Armageddon (Joel 3:12). Further details about the destruction and Armageddon are found in Revelation 6–19.

What happens after the Rapture
during the time of destruction?

Revelation 6:1–17 provides an overview of the post-Rapture era. War and bloodshed dominate verses 3–4 while verses 5–6 depict famine. Verses 7–8 predict widespread death with one-third of the global population perishing. Verses 9–11 reveal the martyrdom of Christians during the tribulation. The subsequent verses (12–17) describe a period marked by dreadful and oppressive terror, indicating the presence of Christians during the tribulation. This raises the question: How can individuals become Christians during the tribulation if all Christians are removed during the Rapture? This inquiry is addressed in the following section.

The possibility of nonbelievers becoming Christians after the Rapture

After the Rapture, nonbelievers have the opportunity to become Christians. The book of Revelation outlines God's plan, involving the dispatch of 144,000 witnesses (Revelation 7:4–8), two witnesses (Revelation 11:1–10), and an angel preaching the gospel (Revelation 14:6) about Jesus Christ. Despite these efforts, many will refuse to repent and instead curse God (Revelation 16:21). Revelation 6:9–11 and 7:9–17 indicate that some individuals will embrace Christianity during the tribulation, albeit at the risk of facing death (Revelation 20:4).

Therefore, the presence of Christians on earth post-Rapture is affirmed.

In conclusion, for Christians raptured before the tribulation, there is the promise of escaping the challenges of an evil and corrupt world and being spared from the tribulation (1 Thessalonians 5:9; Revelation 3:10). However, the outlook is grim for non-Christians entering the tribulation as they will endure severe suffering. Additionally, the absence of Christians to explain the events and guide others on how to become Christian poses a significant challenge. Non-Christians may have to rely on past teachings, sermons, or literature about the Rapture and salvation through belief in Jesus Christ for forgiveness of sins and attainment of eternal life.

CHAPTER 28

The Events of the Tribulation Period

This chapter provides an overview of the events expected to unfold during the tribulation period as described in the book of Revelation and other biblical prophecies. Here's a detailed explanation:

1. *John's ascension (Revelation 4:1–2):* John, representing the church, is taken up to heaven, symbolizing the Rapture of believers before the tribulation.

2. *Antichrist's covenant (Daniel 9:27):* the Antichrist signs a seven-year covenant with Israel, marking the beginning of the tribulation.

3. *First seal - white horse (Revelation 6:1–2):* the Antichrist appears, using diplomacy and promises of peace to establish global dominance.
4. *Second seal - red horse (Revelation 6:3–4):* a world war erupts, causing widespread devastation.
5. *Third seal - black horse (Revelation 6:5–6):* famine and economic collapse follow the war's aftermath.
6. *Fourth seal - pale horse (Revelation 6:7–8):* death and destruction affect a quarter of the world's population.
7. *Martyrdom of believers (Revelation 6:9–11):* those who accept Christ during the tribulation are martyred for their faith.
8. *Sixth seal - cosmic disturbances (Revelation 6:12–17):* catastrophic natural disasters signal the onset of God's wrath.
9. *Seventh seal - seven trumpet judgments (Revelation 8:1–6):* trumpet judgments intensify divine punishment, leading to the "day of His wrath."
10. *First trumpet (Revelation 8:7):* vegetation is devastated by hail, fire, and blood.

11. *Second trumpet (Revelation 8:8–9):* sea life and maritime activities suffer massive destruction.
12. *Third trumpet (Revelation 8:10–11):* freshwater sources are contaminated, leading to widespread death.
13. *Fourth trumpet (Revelation 8:12):* Celestial disturbances darken the skies, exacerbating the tribulation's horrors.
14. *Fifth trumpet - first woe (Revelation 9:1–12):* demonic locusts torment unbelievers, inducing unbearable suffering.
15. *Sixth trumpet - second woe (Revelation 9:13):* demonic cavalry inflicts mass casualties, targeting those who reject God.
16. *Two witnesses (Revelation 11:3–14):* God's witnesses prophesy during the first half of the tribulation, facing opposition but protected by divine power.
17. *Seventh trumpet (Revelation 11:15):* introduces more severe judgments and prepares for the vial judgments.
18. *Destruction of Babylon (Revelation 17:1–18):* the false religious system collapses, setting the stage for further judgments.

19. *Antichrist's resurgence (Revelation 13:1–3):* the Antichrist appears to die but is resurrected, enforcing global worship.
20. *False prophet's influence (Revelation 13:4–10):* the false prophet promotes worship of the Antichrist and implements the mark of the beast.
21. *Vial judgments (Revelation 16:1–21):* intensify God's wrath, causing widespread devastation and prompting defiance among the unrepentant.
22. *Glorious return of Christ (Revelation 19:11–21):* Christ returns triumphantly to establish His kingdom, defeating the forces of evil at the battle of Armageddon.

These events represent a culmination of God's judgment on a rebellious world and the fulfillment of His promises to redeem His people and establish His righteous rule on earth.

CHAPTER 29

What Will Occur When Jesus Ultimately Governs the Earth During the Millennium?

The thousand-year reign of Christ

War, while sometimes necessary, is undeniably a dreadful affair. Even God Himself engages in warfare.

As detailed in the book of Revelation, the world will descend into chaos during the battle of Armageddon, with armies decimated in a nuclear inferno. Gog, Magog, and Rosh will march from the north toward destruction. The Antichrist will face eternal damnation, and an army of two hundred million from the east will invade the Mediterranean region. Such catastrophic events will leave devastation in their wake, requiring seven years to cleanse the land of the ensuing radiation (Revelation 16:12–16).

Revelation also unveils seven seals, symbolizing earth's title deed. While God has seemingly been an absentee landlord, His ultimate plan involves Christ ruling over the earth.

God employs the seven-year Great Tribulation and the battle of Armageddon to eradicate all traces of godless rebellion from the earth. With this cleansing, the one-thousand-year millennium commences (Revelation 20).

Four ways to interpret the Millennium

Premillennialism:

- Christ will physically return to earth before the thousand-year reign.
- Jesus will establish His kingdom, ruling from David's throne in a rebuilt Jerusalem.
- Upon His return, believers will be taken, unbelievers condemned, and eternity will commence.

–   All promises made to Israel will transfer to the church as Israel forfeited them due to unbelief.

Postmillennialism:

–   Advocates believe the world will progressively improve through gospel dissemination, marking the millennial age. After this period, Christ will transport believers to heaven and condemn rejectors.
–   However, the upheavals of two world wars have cast doubt on this view as global conditions show no clear improvement.

Amillennialism:

–   This perspective denies a literal thousand-year reign of Christ on earth and an earthly kingdom of God.
–   God will fulfill His promises and covenants with Israel despite their past spiritual failings.

Pan-Millennialism:

- This viewpoint suggests that everything will eventually *pan* out in the end, implying a lack of concern for specific interpretations.

The significance of whether Christ will reign on earth literally is profound. Personally, I lean toward the premillennial viewpoint for various reasons:

- The central theme of the prophets underscores Israel's preparation for the Messiah's advent and the establishment of His earthly kingdom.
- The essence of Old Testament prophecy revolves around the Messiah's arrival to institute a divine kingdom, with Christ ruling from David's throne.
- God is in the process of restoring all things to their intended order.
- By vindicating righteousness, God will unveil His original design—a unified world under Jesus Christ's governance.
- Just as the seven-year Great Tribulation foreshadows hell on earth, the one-thou-

sand-year reign of Christ offers a glimpse of heaven.

— The millennium serves as a public glorification of the Son of God as depicted in Zechariah 14:16, where survivors from all nations worship the King, the Lord Almighty.

Throughout history, humanity has yearned for a golden age of peace. Philosophers, poets, musicians, politicians, and prophets alike have envisioned it. Yet a misunderstanding led Israel to reject the Messiah, missing their Savior when He arrived in Jerusalem.

The Old Testament foretells a twofold coming of the Messiah. Firstly during the Great Tribulation to gather His saints and, secondly, at the commencement of the thousand-year reign.

His first coming was marked by sacrifice, addressing humanity's sinfulness. Now having dealt with sin, His second coming will establish His earthly kingdom, perhaps imminent.

However, before inaugurating His reign, Jesus must address one final issue: Satan's judgment.

The false prophet, the Antichrist, and unbelievers await judgment at the Great White Throne, where all will be condemned and cast into the Lake of Fire (Revelation 20:11).

Satan himself, the source of all trouble, will be bound for a thousand years, ensuring his deception of nations ceases during the kingdom era (Revelation 20:1–3).

Just before the millennium concludes, Satan will be released briefly to ensure the complete eradication of evil.

*Why does God permit Satan's release
during the millennial reign?*

Martin Bradley offers insight:

- God allows Satan to tempt those who, despite growing up in a perfect God-centric environment, still rebel.
- Just as some angels rebelled in a pristine heavenly realm, a segment of humanity will do likewise.
- Through this final test, God reveals and removes those unwilling to submit to Him, purifying humanity before the advent of the new heaven and new earth.

Despite living in a utopian setting, humans may still rebel, reflecting the innate sinful nature and Satan's influence.

In conclusion, the millennium offers a glimpse of God's intended order, highlighting the necessity of His reign.

CHAPTER 30

What is the Great White Throne Judgment?

In the book of Revelation, there is a mention of a forthcoming judgment known as the Great White Throne Judgment. If you've ever seen judgment scenes depicted in movies, you typically witness a long line of individuals, often surrounded by clouds, waiting for their names to be called. Some have even likened this scene to the portrayal of St. Peter at the pearly gates, checking to see if one's name is on the list for entry into heaven. While these depictions may allow for creative interpretation, they do not diminish the gravity of the impending judgment. It's crucial to understand what the Great White Throne Judgment entails and for whom it is reserved.

What is the Great White Throne Judgment in revelation?

When discussing the Great White Throne Judgment, terms such as Judgment Day or the Last Judgment may be used. This event is referenced in Revelation 20, which we'll explore shortly, but Jesus also alluded to this judgment in the Gospel of John:

> Do not be amazed at this, for a time is coming when all who are in their graves will hear his voice and come out—those who have done what is good will rise to live, and those who have done what is evil will rise to be condemned. (John 5:28–29)

Let's turn to the book of Revelation to see how these two scriptures point to the same event:

> Then I saw a great white throne and him who was seated on it. The earth and the heavens fled from his presence, and there was no place for them. And I saw the

dead, great and small, standing before the throne, and books were opened. Another book was opened, which is the Book of Life. The dead were judged according to what they had done as recorded in the books. The sea gave up the dead that were in it, and death and Hades gave up the dead that were in them, and each person was judged according to what they had done. Then death and Hades were thrown into the lake of fire. The lake of fire is the second death. Anyone whose name was not found written in the Book of Life was thrown into the lake of fire. (Revelation 20:11–15)

Characteristics of the Great White Throne Judgment

When studying Scripture, it's beneficial to ask questions to aid in understanding the passage. These can be referred to as the "W questions"—who, what, where, when, and why. Let's apply these to this passage:

Who will be judged? The Great White Throne Judgment is reserved for unbelievers, not believers. How do we know this? A preceding passage in Revelation reveals it:

> I saw thrones on which were seated those who had been given authority to judge. And I saw the souls of those who had been beheaded because of their testimony about Jesus and because of the Word of God. They had not worshiped the beast or its image and had not received its mark on their foreheads or their hands. They came to life and reigned with Christ a thousand years. (The rest of the dead did not come to life until the thousand years were ended.) This is the first resurrection. Blessed and holy are those who share in the first resurrection. The second death has no power over them, but they will be

> priests of God and of Christ and
> will reign with him for a thou-
> sand years. (Revelation 20:4–6)

Those present at and participating in the Great White Throne Judgment are those who were not resurrected at the beginning of the millennial period, constituting the second resurrection. These individuals did not partake in the first resurrection, signifying that they did not share in the blessings and holiness afforded to believers.

When and where will they be judged? This judgment will occur after Christ's thousand-year reign on earth. These individuals will have already perished and will await judgment during this period until their final trial. Similar to being held in custody until a trial date in a criminal case, these individuals will remain in Hades until summoned to appear before God for judgment. Their trial and subsequent judgment will occur before the throne of God, represented by the Great White Throne.

What will they be judged for? According to Revelation, they will be judged based on their deeds as recorded in the books. Each person will be held accountable for their actions and sins.

Why are they being judged? This judgment results from their rejection of Christ as their Savior and their choice to bear the penalty for their sins themselves. As God is just, holy, and righteous, all sin demands a penalty. Those who accept Christ have their sin's penalty transferred to Him while those who reject Him carry the burden of their sins themselves, facing severe consequences.

Does the Bible say that there's one judgment or two judgments?

Jesus referred to two distinct judgments: one for believers and one for unbelievers. For believers, there is the judgment seat of Christ, where rewards and punishments are meted out based on their deeds after accepting Christ as Savior: "For we must all appear before the judgment seat of Christ so that each of us may receive what is due us for the things done while in the body, whether good or bad" (2 Corinthians 5:10).

This judgment is not for salvation but for the evaluation of works performed after accepting salvation. Paul elaborates on this in 1 Corinthians:

> If anyone builds on this foundation using gold, silver, costly

> stones, wood, hay or straw, their work will be shown for what it is, because the day will bring it to light. It will be revealed with fire, and the fire will test the quality of each person's work. If what has been built survives, the builder will receive a reward. If it is burned up, the builder will suffer loss but yet will be saved—even though only as one escaping through the flames. (1 Corinthians 3:12–15)

Even if one's works are burned up, salvation remains secure through faith in Christ.

Distinguishing this from the Great White Throne Judgment in Revelation, the latter signifies a judgment of eternal destiny, where mercy and grace are no longer extended. It's a final pronouncement based on the individual's guilt, devoid of a trial.

The seriousness of the Great White Throne Judgment

The Great White Throne Judgment is a solemn event, carrying significant weight. There is no celebration for those facing this judgment, and believers should not rejoice when contemplating the fate of those who died without knowing Christ. For them, this judgment awaits as Scripture reminds us: "And as it is appointed for men to die once, but after this the judgment" (Hebrews 9:27 NKJV).

Death is inevitable, leading to judgment. The question remains: Will it be the judgment seat of Christ or the Great White Throne? Those in Christ need not fear the latter. This knowledge should not only bring rejoicing but also serve as motivation to share the gospel, seeking to rescue as many as possible from this fate. This is the calling of every believer, spurred by the sobering reality of final judgment.

CHAPTER 31

What Is the Concept of the New Heaven and New Earth?

Revelation 21 presents a compelling prophecy regarding the future destiny of our world. John describes a vision where he sees "a new heaven and a new earth, for the first heaven and the first earth had passed away. Also, there was no more sea" (Revelation 21:1). But what does this signify? What will the new heaven and earth entail, and what becomes of our current existence?

Understanding the time frame of
the new heaven and earth

To grasp this prophecy, we must comprehend its contextual time frame. The book of Revelation outlines events leading up to Christ's return to earth and the subsequent establishment of God's kingdom. Following Christ's return, there will be a one-thousand-year reign with Him and His glorified saints. These saints—resurrected to immortal, spirit life—will usher in the first resurrection (1 Corinthians 15:50–52; Revelation 20:4, 6).

After this initial millennial reign, Revelation 20:5 indicates a resurrection of all other humans who have lived and died throughout history. These individuals will face judgment (Revelation 20:12–13). By the conclusion of this period of judgment, those who embrace God's way will be granted eternal life, while those who reject it will face the "lake of fire" (Revelation 20:15), symbolizing final and irreversible condemnation.

Understanding the Lake of Fire

The Lake of Fire, depicted as expanding in 2 Peter 3, signifies the destruction of the ungodly. This fiery end leads to the dissolution of the heavens and the earth (2 Peter 3:7, 10). The physical elements will melt away, paving the way for the emergence of new heavens and a new earth where righteousness reigns (2 Peter 3:13).

The nature of the new heaven(s) and earth

The term "new" in Greek (*kainos*) denotes a state of freshness rather than mere chronological newness. Whether this entails a complete recreation of the earth or a purification of its surface, the outcome remains a planet remade by God. This transformation is likened to putting on a new garment (Psalm 102:25–26), suggesting a profound renewal.

In Revelation 21:1, John describes seeing a new heaven and a new earth, signifying a fresh state of existence. This passage emphasizes the passing away of the former, implying its cessation.

Purpose of the new heaven and earth

Contrary to traditional beliefs, where heaven is viewed as the ultimate reward, Scripture reveals that the righteous will inherit the earth (Matthew 5:5). Thus, the concept of a new heaven and earth underscores God's plan for an eternal dwelling place where righteousness prevails.

Phillip Compton was born in Diamond Bar, California, in 1968, into a family deeply entrenched in the Christian faith. His father, David R. Compton, a prominent figure in the original Jesus Movement, laid the foundation for Phillip's spiritual journey.

Military service

In 1986, Phillip answered the call to serve his country by enlisting in the United States Marine Corps. For seven years, he dedicated himself to the corps, serving in artillery and embodying the values of honor, courage, and commitment.

Spiritual formation

After his military service, Phillip pursued theological studies at Calvary Chapel, under the mentorship of Pastor Chuck Smith. This period of education and spiritual growth shaped his understanding of Scripture and his calling to ministry.

Pastoral ministry

Phillip's passion for serving others led him to become an associate pastor at various churches. His experiences in this role equipped him with the skills and compassion necessary to guide and support congregations in their spiritual journeys.

Leadership at Calvary Harvest Ministry

Phillip's journey culminated in his appointment as the pastor of Calvary Harvest Ministry, where he continues to lead with wisdom, compassion, and a deep-rooted faith. Under his leadership, the ministry thrives as a beacon of hope and a source of spiritual nourishment for the community.

Legacy

Phillip Compton's life is a testament to faith, service, and unwavering commitment. From his humble beginnings in Diamond Bar to his leadership at Calvary Harvest Ministry, he exemplifies the transformative power of faith and the profound impact of a life dedicated to serving others.